Nightgown and other stories

The Corgi Series *Writing from Wales*

1. Dannie Abse, *Touch Wood*
2. Idris Davies, *A Carol for the Coalfield*
3. Mike Jenkins, *Laughter Tangled in Thorn*
4. *War*, an anthology edited by Dewi Roberts
5. Alun Richards, *Scandalous Thoughts*
6. Alun Lewis, *The Sentry*
7. Tony Curtis, *Considering Cassandra*
8. *Love*, an anthology edited by Dewi Roberts
9. Raymond Garlick, *The Delphic Voyage*
10. Rhys Davies, *Nightgown*
11. Sheenagh Pugh, *What If This Road*
12. *Places*, an anthology edited by Dewi Roberts
13. Leslie Norris, *Water*
14. T. H. Jones, *Lucky Jonah*
15. Paul Henry, *The Breath of Sleeping Boys*
16. *Work*, an anthology edited by Dewi Roberts
17. Harri Webb, *The Stone Face*
18. Geraint Goodwin, *The Shearing*
19. John Ormond, *Boundaries*
20. *Landscapes*, an anthology edited by Dewi Roberts
21. Glyn Jones, *The Common Path*
22. Gwyn Thomas, *Land! Land!*
23. Emyr Humphreys, *The Rigours of Inspection*
24. *Death*, an anthology edited by Dewi Roberts

The Corgi Series  *Writing from Wales*

RHYS DAVIES

Nightgown and other stories

Series editor
Meic Stephens
Emeritus Professor of Welsh Writing in English
University of Glamorgan

Carreg Gwalch Cyf.

© The estate of Rhys Davies

*All rights reserved. No part of this publication
may be reproduced or transmitted, in any form
or by any means, without permission.*

ISBN: 0-86381-710-6

Cover design: Sian Parri

*Carreg Gwalch Cyf. wishes to acknowledge the help of
Martin Tinney Gallery, Cardiff (www.artwales.com)
in supplying a slide of the artwork for the cover.*

Logo design: Dylan Williams

*First published in 2003 by
Carreg Gwalch Cyf., 12 Iard yr Orsaf, Llanrwst,
Wales LL26 0EH
✆ 01492 642031   ▤ 01492 641502
✉ books@carreg-gwalch.co.uk
website: www.carreg-gwalch.co.uk*

*Supported by an 'Arts for All' Lottery grant
from the Arts Council of Wales*

*Carreg Gwalch Cyf. acknowledges the
co-operation of the Rhys Davies Estate
in the publication of these stories.*

Contents

Introduction 6

Nightgown 9

The Dark World 26

The Last Struggle 38

The Public House 58

Canute 68

Fear 85

For further reading 93

Rhys Davies (1901-78)

Rhys Davies, novelist and short-story writer, was born on 9 November 1901 in the mining village of Blaenclydach, in a side-valley of the Rhondda Fawr, not far from Tonypandy. The house where he was born, 6 Clydach Road, now marked by a commemorative plaque, was a grocer's shop known as Royal Stores; across the road stands the Central Hotel, which often appears in his stories as the Jubilee. Rees Vivian Davies, as he was christened, was the fourth child of the village grocer and his wife. His parents' status as shopkeepers set the family apart from a community that depended almost entirely on the digging of coal at two local pits, the Cambrian and a drift-mine, known as the Gorki, quite close to where they lived. But the shop's daily routine brought the boy into close contact with the village people, especially the womenfolk, for whom he felt a deep affection and whose gossip he relished. The Cambrian mine was the focus for the Tonypandy riots of 1910, which he was to write about in his autobiography, *Print of a Hare's Foot*.

At Porth County School young Davies did little to distinguish himself academically and left at the age of fourteen, much to the chagrin of his parents, and began to help behind the counter at Royal Stores. He also read avidly, mainly Chekhov and

Maupassant, and made his first adolescent attempts at writing poems and stories. 'I always think of this period of my life as a burial,' he commented, 'with myself lying somnolent in a coffin, but visually aware of the life going on around me, and content to wait until the time came for me to rise and be myself.' For him that meant coming to terms with his homosexuality, a painful process which made life in the Rhondda unbearable. Daunted by the grime and coarseness of life in the Valley, and by what he saw as the narrowness of its chapel culture, he went to live for a while in Cardiff, where he found work in a corn-merchant's warehouse, and soon afterwards left Wales for London. He was never to live permanently in the Rhondda again, but its ethos had marked him indelibly and provided him with an inexhaustible source of material for his writing.

For the next fifty years Rhys Davies, with unswerving devotion, lived as a full-time writer, publishing nineteen novels, three novellas, two books about Wales, an autobiography, and about a hundred stories in a dozen main collections. His life, which he shared with no other person, was without great incident, except perhaps for a few months spent in the south of France, where he was befriended by D.H. Lawrence. A lifelong smoker, he died of lung-cancer in London on 21 August 1978.

Nightgown

I

She had married Walt after a summer courtship during which they had walked together in a silence like aversion.

Coming of a family of colliers, too, the smell of the hulking young man tramping to her when she stepped out of an evening was the sole smell of men. He would have the faintly scowling look which presently she, too, acquired. He half resented having to go about their business, but still his feet impelled him to her street corner and made him wait until, closed-faced and glancing sideways threateningly, she came out of her father's house. They walked wordless on the grit beside the railway track, his mouth open as though in a perpetual yawn. For courting she had always worn a new lilac dress out of a proper draper's shop. This dress was her last fling in that line.

She got married in it, and they took one of the seven-and-six-penny slices of the long blocks of concreted stone whipping round a slope and called Bryn Hyfryd – that is, Pleasant Hill. Like her father, Walt was a pub collier, not chapel.

The big sons had arrived with unchanged regularity, each of the same heavy poundage. When the sex of the fifth was told her, she turned her face sullenly to the wall and did not look at him for some time. And he was her last. She was to have no companionable daughter after all, to dote on when the men were in the pit. As the sons grew, the house became so obstreperously male that she began to lose nearly all feminine attributes and was apt to wear a man's cap and her sons' shoes, socks, and mufflers to run out to the shop. Her expression became tight as a fist, her jaw jutted out like her men's and like them she only used her voice when it was necessary, though sometimes she would clang out at them with a criticism they did not understand. They would only scowl the family scowl.

For a while she had turned in her shut-up way to Trevor, her last-born. She wanted him to be small and delicate – she had imagined he was of different mould from his brothers – and she had dim ideas of his putting his hand to something more elegant than a pick in the pits. He grew into the tall, gruff image of his brothers. Yet still, when the time came for him to leave school at fourteen, she had bestirred herself, cornering him and speaking in her sullen way:

'Trevor, you don't want to go to that dirty old pit, do you? Plenty of other things to do. One white face let me have coming home to me now.'

He had set up a hostile bellow at once. 'I'm going to the pit. Dad's going to ask his haulier for me.' He stared at her in fear. 'To the pits I'm going. You let me alone.' He dreaded her hard but seeking approaches; his brothers would poke jeering fun at him, asking him if his napkins were pinned on all right, it was as if they tried to destroy her need of him, snatching him away.

She had even attempted to wring help from her husband: 'Walt, why can't Trevor be something else? What do I want with six men in the pit? One collier's more work in the house than four clean-job men.'

'Give me a shilling, 'ooman,' he said, crossing his red-spotted white muffler, 'and don't talk daft.' And off he went to the Miskin Arms.

So one bitter January morning she had seen her last-born leave the house with her other men, pit trousers on his lengthening legs and a gleaming new jack and food tin under his arm. From that day he had ranged up inextricably with his brothers, sitting down with them at four o'clock to bacon and potatoes, even the same quantity of everything, and never derided by them again. She accepted his loss, as she was bound to do, though her jutting jaw seemed more bony, thrust out like a lonely hand into the world's air.

They were all on the day shift in the pits, and in a way she had good luck, for not one met with any accidents to speak of, they worked regular, and had no fancies to stay at home because of a pain in big toe or ear lobe, like some lazybones. So there ought to have been good money in the house. But there wasn't.

They ate most of it, with the rest for drinking. Bacon was their chief passion, and it must be of the best cut. In the shop, where she was never free of debt, nearly every day she would ask for three pounds of thick rashers when others would ask for one, and if Mr Griffiths would drop a hint, looking significantly at his thick ledger, saying: 'Three pounds, Mrs Rees, *again*?' her reply was always: 'I've got big men to feed.' As if that was sufficient explanation for all debt and she could do nothing about it; there were big, strapping men in the world and they had to be fed.

Except with one neighbour, she made no kind of real contact with anyone outside her home. And not much inside it. Of the middle height and bonily skimped of body, she seemed extinguished by the assembly of big males she had put into the world off her big husband. Peering out surly from under the poke of her man's cap, she never went beyond the main street of the vale, though as a child she had been once to the seaside, in a buff straw hat ringed with daisies.

Gathered in their pit-dirt for the important four-o'clock meal, with bath pans and hot foods steaming in the fireplace, the little kitchen was crowded as the Black Hole of Calcutta. None of the sons, not even the eldest, looked like marrying, though sometimes, like a shoving parent bird, she would try to push them out of the nest. One or two of them set up brief associations with girls which never seemed to come properly to anything. They were the kind that never marry until the entertainments of youth, such as football, whippet-racing, and beer, have palled at last. She would complain to her next-door-up neighbour that she had no room to put down even a thimble.

This neighbour, Mrs Lewis – the other neighbours set her bristling – was her only friend in the place, though the two never entered each other's house. In low voices they conversed over the back wall, exchanging all the eternal woes of women in words of cold, knowledgeable judgment that God Himself could have learnt from. To Mrs Lewis's remark that Trevor, her last, going to work in the pits ought to set her on her feet now, she said automatically, but sighing for once: 'I've got big men to feed.' That fact was the core of her world. Trevor's money, even when he began to earn a man's wage, was of no advantage. Still she was in debt in the shop. The six men were profitless; the demands of their insides made them white elephants.

So now, at fifty, still she could not sit down on the sofa for an hour and dream of a day by the seaside with herself in a clean new dress at last and a draper's-shop hat fresh as a rose.

But often in the morning she skulked to London House, the draper's on the corner of the main road, and stopped for a moment to peer sideways into the window where two wax women, one fair and one dark, stood dressed in all the latest fashions and smiling a pink, healthy smile. Looking beautiful beyond compare, these two ladies were now more living to her than her old dream of a loving daughter. They had no big men to feed and, poised in their eternal shade, smiled leisurely above their furs and silk blouses. It was her treat to see them, as she stood glancing out from under Enoch's thrown-away cap, her toe-sprouting shoes unlaced and her skirt of drab flannel hanging scarecrow. Every other week they wore something new. The days when Mr Roberts the draper changed their outfits, the sight of the new wonders remained in her eyes until the men arrived home from the pit.

Then one morning she was startled to find the fair wax lady attired in a wonderful white silk nightgown, flowing down over the legs most richly and trimmed with lace at bosom and cuffs. That anyone could wear such luxuriance in bed struck her at first like a blow in the face. Besides, it was a shock to see the grand lady standing there undressed, as you might say, in public. But, staring into the window, she was suddenly thrilled.

She went home feeling this new luxury round her like a sweet, clean silence. Where no men were.

II

At four o'clock they all clattered in, Walt and her five swart sons, flinging down food tins and jacks. The piled heaps of bacon and potatoes were ready. On the scrubbed table were six large plates, cutlery, mugs, and a loaf, a handful of lumpy salt chucked down in the middle. They ate their meal before washing, in their pit-dirt, and the six black faces, red mouths and white eyes gleaming, could be differentiated only by a mother.

Jaw stuck out, she worked about the table, shifting on to each plate four thick slices of bacon, a stream of sizzling fat, ladles of potatoes and tinned tomatoes. They poked their knives into the heap of salt, scattered it over the plate, and began. Lap of tongue around food was their only noise for a while. She poured the thick black tea out of a battered enamel pot big enough for a palace or a workhouse.

At last a football match was mentioned, and what somebody said last night in the Miskin taproom about that little whippet. She got the tarts ready, full-sized plates of them, and they slogged at these; the six plates were left naked in a trice. Oddments followed: cheese, cake, and jams. They only stopped eating when she stopped producing.

She said, unexpectedly: 'Shouldn't be surprised if you'd all sit there till doomsday, 'long as I went on bringing food without stoppage.'

'Aye,' said Ivor. 'What about a tin of peaches?'

Yet not one of them, not even her middle-aged husband, had a protuberant belly or any other signs of large eating. Work in the pit kept them sinewy and their sizes as nature intended. Similarly, they could have drunk beer from buckets, like horses, without looking it. Everything three or four times the nice quantities eaten by most people, but no luxuries except that the sons never spread jam thinly on bread like millionaires' sons but in fat dabs, and sometimes they demanded pineapple chunks for breakfast as if they were kings or something. She wondered sometimes that they did not grind up the jam pots, too, in their strong white shiny teeth; but Trevor, the youngest, had the rights to lick the pots, and thrust down his tongue almost to the bottom.

At once, after the meal, the table was shoved back. She dragged in the wooden tub before the fire. Her husband always washed first, taking the clean water. He slung his pit clothes to the corner, belched, and stepped into the tub. He did not seem in a hurry this afternoon. He stood and rubbed up his curls – still black and crisp after fifty years – and bulged the muscle of his black right arm. 'Look there,' he said, 'you pups, if a muscle like that you got at my age, men you can call yourselves.'

Ranged about the kitchen, waiting for their bath turn with cigarette stuck to red-licked lower lip, the five sons looked variously derisive, secure in their own bone and muscle. But they said nothing; the father had a certain power, lordly in his maturity. He stood there naked, handsome, and well-endowed; he stood musing for a bit, liking the hot water round his feet and calves. But his wife, out and in with towels, shirts, and buckets, had heard his remark. With the impatience that had seemed to writhe about her ever since they had clattered in, she cried: 'What are you standing there for showing off, you big ram! Wash yourself, man, and get away with you.'

He took no notice. One after the other the sons stripped; after the third bath the water was changed, being then thick and heavy as mud. They washed each other's back, and she scuttled in and out, like a dark, irritated crab this afternoon, her angry voice nipping at them. When Ieuan, the eldest and six foot two, from where he was standing in the tub spat across into a pan of fresh water on the fire, in a sudden fury she snatched up the dirty coal-shovel and gave him a ringing smack on his washed behind. Yet the water was only intended for the dirt-crusted tub. He scowled; she shouted: 'You blackguard, you keep your spit for public-house floors.'

After she had gone into the scullery, Trevor, waiting his turn, grunted: 'What's the matter with the old woman today?' Ieuan stepped out of the tub. The shovel blow might have been the tickle of a feather. But Trevor advised him: 'Better wash your best face again; that shovel's left marks.'

From six o'clock onwards one by one they left the house, all, including Walt, in a navy-blue serge suit, muffler, cap, and yellowish-brown shoes, their faces glistening pale from soap. They strutted away on their long, easy legs to their various entertainments, though with their heads somehow down in a kind of ducking. Their tallness made it a bit awkward for themselves in some of the places down in the pits.

Left alone with the piles of crusted pit clothes, all waiting to be washed or dried of their sweat, she stood taking a cup of tea and nibbling a piece of bread, looking out of the window. Except on Sundays her men seldom saw her take a meal, though even on Sunday she never ate bacon. There was a month or two of summer when she appeared to enjoy a real plate of something, for she liked kidney beans and would eat a whole plateful, standing with her back to the room and looking out of the window towards the distant mountain brows under the sky, as if she was thinking of Heaven. Her fourth son Emlyn said to her once: 'Your Sunday feed lasts you all the week, does it? Or a good guzzle you have when we're in the pit?'

She stood thinking till her head hurt. The day died on the mountain-tops. Where was the money coming from, with them everlasting pushing expensive bacon into their red mouths? The clock ticked.

Suddenly, taking a coin from a secret place and pulling on a cap, she hurried out. A spot burning in her cheeks, she shot into the corner draper's just as he was about to close, and, putting out her jaw, panted to old Roberts: 'What's the price of that silk nightgown on the lady in the window?'

After a glance at the collier's wife in man's cap and skirt rough as an old mat, Roberts said crossly: ' A price you can't afford, so there!' But when she seemed to mean business he told her it was seventy bob and elevenpence and he hoped that the pit manager's wife or the doctor's would fancy it.

She said defiantly: 'You sell it to me. A bob or more a week I'll pay you, and you keep it till I've finished the amount. Take it out of the window now at once and lay it by. Go on now, fetch it out.'

'What's the matter with you!' he shouted testily, as though he was enraged as well as astonished at her wanting a silk nightgown. 'What d'you want it for?'

'Fetch it out,' she threatened, 'or my husband Walt Rees I'll send to you quick.' The family of big, fighting males was well-known in the streets. After some more palaver Roberts agreed to accept her instalments and, appeased, she insisted on waiting until he had undraped the wax lady in the window. With a bony, trembling finger she felt the soft white silk for a second and hurried out of the shop.

III

How she managed to pay for the nightgown in less than a year was a mystery, for she had never a penny to spare, and a silver coin in the house in the middle of the week was rare as a Christian in England. But regularly she shot into the draper's and opened her grey fist to Roberts. Sometimes she demanded to see the nightgown, frightened that he might have sold it for quick money to someone else, though Roberts would shout at her: 'What's the matter with you? Packed up safe it is.'

One day she braved his wrath and asked if she could take it away, promising faithful to keep up the payments. But he exclaimed: 'Be off! Enough tradesmen here been ruined by credit. Buying silk nightgowns indeed! What next?'

She wanted the nightgown in the house; she was fearful it would never be hers in time. Her instinct told her to be swift. So she hastened, robbing still further her own stomach and in tiny lots even trying to rob the men's, though they would scowl and grumble if even the rind was off their bacon. But at last, when March winds blew down off the mountains so that she had to wrap round her scraggy chest the gaunt shawl in which her five lusty babies had been nursed, she paid the last instalment. Her chin and cheeks blue in excitement, she took the parcel home when the men were in the pit.

Locking the door, she washed her hands, opened the parcel, and sat with the silk delicately in her hands, sitting quiet for half an hour at last, her eyes come out in a gleam from her dark face, brilliant. Then she hid the parcel down under household things in a drawer which the men never used.

A week or two later, when she was asking for the usual three pounds of bacon at the shop, Mr Griffith said to her, stern: 'What about the old debts, now then? Pity you don't pay up, instead of buying silk nightgowns. Cotton is good enough for my mussus to sleep in, and you lolling in silk, and don't pay for all your bacon and other things. Pineapple chunks every day. Hoo!' And he glared.

'Nightgown isn't for *my* back,' she snapped. 'A wedding present for a relation it is.' But she was a bit winded that the draper had betrayed her secret to his fellow tradesman.

He grumbled: 'Don't know what to do with all you take out of my shop. Bacon every day enough to feed a funeral, and tins of fruit and salmons by the dozen. Eat for fun, do you?'

'I've got big men to feed.' She scowled, as usual.

Yet she seemed less saturnine as she sweated over the fireplace and now never once exclaimed an irritation at some clumsiness of the men. Even when, nearly at Easter, she began to go bad, no complaint came from her, and of course the men did not notice, for still their bacon was always ready and the tarts as many, their bath water hot, and evening shirts ironed.

On Easter Bank Holiday, when she stopped working for a while because the men had gone to whippet races over in Maerdy Valley, she had time to think of her pains. She felt as if the wheels of several coal wagons had gone over her body, though there were no feeling at all in her legs. When the men arrived home at midnight, boozed up, there were hot faggots for them, basting pans savoury full, and their pit clothes were all ready for the morning. She attended on them in a slower fashion, her face closed and her body shorter, because her legs had gone bowed. But they never noticed, jabbering of the whippets.

Mrs Lewis next door said she ought to stay in bed for a week. She replied that the men had to be fed.

A fortnight later, just before they arrived home from the pit and the kitchen was hot as a furnace, her legs kicked themselves in the air, the full frying-pan in her hand went flying, and when they came in they found her black-faced on the floor with the rashers of bacon all about her. She died in the night as the district nurse was wetting her lips with water. Walt, who was sleeping in a chair downstairs, went up too late to say farewell.

Because the house was upside down as a result, with the men not fed properly, none of them went to work in the morning. At nine o'clock Mrs Lewis next door, for the first time after thirty years of back-wall friendship with the deceased, stepped momentously into the house. But she had received her instructions weeks ago. After a while she called down from upstairs to the men sitting uneasy in the kitchen: 'Come up; she is ready now.'

They slunk up in procession, six big men, with their heads ducked, disturbed out of the rhythm of their daily life of work, food, and pub. And entering the room for the last view, they stared in surprise.

A stranger lay on the bed ready for her coffin. A splendid, shiny, white silk nightgown flowing down over her feet, with rich lace frilling bosom and hands, she lay like a lady taking a rest, clean and comfortable. So much they stared, it might have been an angel shining there. But her face jutted stern, bidding no approach to the contented peace she had found.

The father said, cocking his head respectfully: 'There's a fine 'ooman she looks. Better than when

I married her!'

'A grand nightshirt,' mumbled Enoch. 'That nurse brought it in her bag?'

'A shroud they call it,' said Emlyn.

'In with the medical benefits it is,' said his father soberly. 'Don't they dock us enough every week from our wages?'

After gazing for a minute longer at the white apparition, lying there so majestically unknown, they filed downstairs. There Mrs Lewis awaited them. 'Haven't you got no 'ooman relation to come in and look after you?' she demanded.

The father shook his head, scowling in effort to concentrate on a new problem. Big, black-curled, and still vigorous, he sat among his five strapping sons who, like him, smelt of the warm, dark energy of life. He said: 'A new missus I shall have to be looking for. Who is there about, Mrs Lewis, that is respectable and can cook for us and see to our washings? My boys I got to think about. A nice little widow or something you know of that would marry a steady working chap? A good home is waiting for her by here, though a long day it'll be before I find one that can feed and clean us like the one above; *she* worked regular as a clock, fair play to her.'

'I don't know as I would recommend any 'ooman,' said Mrs Lewis with rising colour.

'Pity you're not a widow! Ah well, I must ask

the landlady of the Miskin if she knows of one,' he said, concentrated.

A Finger in Every Pie (1942)

The Dark World

'Where can we go tonight?' Jim asked. Once again it was raining. The rows of houses in the valley bed were huddled in cold grey mist. Beyond them the mountains prowled unseen. The iron street lamps spurted feeble jets of light. There were three weeks to go before Christmas. They stood in a chapel doorway and idly talked, their feet splashed by the rain.

Thomas said: 'There's someone dead up in Calfaria Terrace.'

'Shall we go to see him?' Jim suggested immediately.

They had not seen any corpses for some weeks. One evening they had seen five, and so for a while the visits had lost their interest. When on these expeditions they would search through the endless rows of houses for windows covered with white sheets, the sign that death was within, and when a house was found thus, they would knock at the door and respectfully ask if they might see the dead. Only once they were denied, and this had been at a villa, not a common house. Everywhere else they had been taken to the parlour or bedroom where the corpse lay, sometimes in a coffin, and allowed a few seconds' stare. Sometimes the woman of the house, or maybe a daughter, would whisper: 'You knew him, did you?' Or, if the deceased was a child: 'You were in the same school?' They would nod gravely. Often they had walked three or four miles through the valley searching out these dramatic houses. It was Jim who always knocked at the door and said, his cap in his hand: 'We've come to pay our respects, mum.'

At the house in Calfaria Terrace they were two in a crowd. The dead had been dead only a day and neighbours were also paying their respects, as was the custom: there was quite a procession to the upstairs room. The corpse was only a very old man, and his family seemed quite cheerful about it. Thomas heard the woman of the house whisper busily on the landing to a neighbour in a shawl: 'That black blouse you had on the line, Jinny, it'll be a help. The 'surance won't cover the fun'ral, and you know Emlyn lost four days in the pit last week. Still, gone he is now, and there'll be room for a lodger.' And, entreatingly: 'You'll breadcrumb the ham for me, Jinny? . . . I 'ont forget you when you're in trouble of your own.' The dead old man lay under a patchwork quilt. His face was set in an expression of mild surprise. Thomas noticed dried soapsuds in his ear. Four more people came into the bedroom and the two boys were almost hustled out. No one had taken any particular notice of them. Downstairs they asked a skinny cruel-looking young woman for a glass of water and to their pleased astonishment she gave them each a glass of small beer.

'It didn't seem as though he was dead at all,' Jim said, as if cheated. 'Let's look for more. In November there's a lot of them. They get bronchitis and consumption.'

'It was like a wedding,' Thomas said. Again they stood in a doorway and looked with vacant boredom through the black curtains of rain sweeping the valley.

'My mother had a new baby last night,' Jim suddenly blurted out, frowning. But when Thomas asked what kind it was, Jim said he didn't know yet. But he knew that there were nine of them now, beside his father and mother and two lodgers. He did not complain. But of late he had been expressing an ambition to go to sea when he left school, instead of going to the colliery.

Jim, in the evenings, was often pushed out of home by his mother, a bitter black-browed woman who was never without a noisy baby. Jim's father was Irish, a collier of drunken reputation in the place, and the whole family was common as a clump of dock. Thomas's mother sometimes made one or two surprised remarks at his association with Jim. They shared a double desk in school. Occasionally Thomas expressed disgust at Jim's unwashed condition.

Again they set out down the streets, keeping a

sharp lookout for white sheets in the windows. After a while they found a house so arrayed, yellow blobs of candle-light like sunflowers shining through the white of the parlour. Jim knocked and respectfully made his request to a big creaking woman in black. But she said gently: 'Too late you are. The coffin was screwed down after tea today. Funeral is tomorrow. The wreaths you would like to see?'

Jim hesitated, looking back enquiringly over his shoulder at Thomas. Without speaking, both rejected this invitation, and with mumbled thanks they backed away. 'No luck tonight,' Jim muttered.

'There was the small beer,' Thomas reminded him. A wind had jumped down from the mountains and as they scurried on it unhooked a faulty door of a street-lamp and blew out the wispy light. When they had reached the bottom of the vale the night was black and rough and moaning, the rain stinging hot on cheeks and hands like whips. Here was a jumbled mass of swarthy and bedraggled dwellings, huddled like a stagnant meeting of bats. A spaniel, dragging her swollen belly, whined out to them from under a bony bush. She sounded lost and confused and exhausted with the burden that weighted her to earth. In the dark alley-ways they found a white sheet. A winter silence was here, the black houses were glossy in the rain. No one was about.

'Let's go back,' whispered Thomas. 'It's wet and late.'

'There's one here,' Jim protested. 'After coming all this way!' And he tapped at the door, which had no knocker.

The door was opened and in a shaft of lamplight stood a man's shape, behind him a warm fire-coloured interior, for the door opened on to the living room. Jim made his polite request, and the man silently stood aside. They walked into the glow.

But the taste of death was in the house, true and raw. A very bent old woman in a black cardigan clasped at her stingy throat with a geranium brooch, sat nodding before the fire. Thomas was staring at the man, who had cried out:

'It's Thomas!' He sat down heavily on a chair: 'Oh, Thomas!' he said in a wounded voice. His stricken face was though he were struggling to repudiate a new pain. A tall handsome man, known to Thomas as Elias, his face had the grey tough pallor of the underground worker.

The boy stood silent in the shock of the recognition and the suspicion prowling about his mind. He could not speak, he dare not ask. Then fearfully the man said:

'You've come to see Gwen, have you! All this way. Only yesterday I was wondering if your mother had heard. You've come to see her!'

'Yes,' Thomas muttered, his head bent. Jim stood waiting, shifting his feet. The old woman kept on nodding her head. Her son said to her loudly, his voice sounding out in suffering, not having conquered this new reminder of the past years. 'Mam, this is Thomas, Mrs Morgan's boy. You remember? That Gwen was fond of.'

The old woman dreadfully began to weep. Her face, crumpled and brown as a dead rose, winced and shook out slow difficult tears. 'Me it ought to have been,' she said with a thin obsession. 'No sense in it, no sense at all.'

Thomas glanced secretly at Elias, to see if his emotion had abated. Three years ago he used to carry notes from Elias to Gwen, who had been the servant at home. It seemed to him that Elias and Gwen were always quarrelling. Elias used to stand for hours on the street corner until he came past, hurry up to him and say hoarsely: 'Thomas, please will you take this to Gwen.' In the kitchen at home, Gwen would always toss her head on the receipt of a note, and sometimes she indignantly threw them on the fire without reading them . . . But Gwen used to be nice. She always kept back for him, after her evening out, some of Elias's chocolates. Once or twice she had obtained permission to take him to the music-hall and gloriously he had sat between her and Elias, watching the marvellous conjurors and the women in tights who heaved their bejewelled bosoms as they sang funny songs. But Elias, he had felt, had not welcomed those intrusions. After a long time, Gwen had married him. But before she left to do this, she had wept every day for a week, her strong kind face wet and gloomy. His mother had given her a handsome parlour clock and Gwen had tearfully said she would never wind it as it would last longer if unused. Then gradually she had disappeared, gone into her new married life down the other end of the valley.

Elias looked older, older and thinner. Thomas kept his gaze away from him as much as possible. He felt shy at being drawn into the intimacy of all this grief. The old woman kept on quavering. At last Elias said, quietly now: 'You will come upstairs to see her, Thomas. And your friend.' He opened a door at the staircase and, tall and gaunt, waited for them to pass. Thomas walked past him unwillingly, his stomach gone cold. He did not want to go upstairs. But he thought that Elias would take a refusal hardly. Jim, silent and impassive, followed with politely quiet steps.

In a small, small bedroom with a low ceiling two candles were burning. A bunch of snowy chrysanthemums stood on a table beside a pink covered bed. Elias had preceded them and now he lifted a starched white square of cloth from off the head and shoulders of the dead.

She was lying tucked in the bed as if quietly asleep. The bedroom was so small there was nowhere else to look. Thomas looked, and started with a terrified surprise. The sheets were folded back, low under Gwen's chest, and cradled in her arms was a pale waxen doll swathed in white. A doll! His amazement passed into terror. He could not move, and the scalp of his head contracted as though an icy wind passed over it. Surely that wasn't a baby, that pale stiff thing Gwen was nursing against her quiet breast! Elias was speaking in a hoarse whisper, and while he spoke he stroked a fold of the bed-clothes with a grey hand.

'Very hard it was, Thomas, Gwen going like this. The two of them, I was in the pit, and they sent for me. But she had gone before I was here, though old Watkins let me come in his car . . . I didn't see her, Thomas, and she asked for me—' His voice broke, and Thomas in his anguish of terror, saw him drop beside the bed and bury his face in the bed.

It was too much. Thomas wanted to get away; he wanted to run, away from the close narrow room, from the man shuddering beside the bed, from the figure in the bed that had been the warm Gwen, from the strange creature in her arms that looked as though it had never been warm. The terror became a nightmare menace coming nearer

. . . Unconsciously he jerked his way out to the landing. Jim followed; he looked oppressed.

'Let's clear off,' he whispered nervously.

They went downstairs. The old woman was brewing tea, and in the labour seemed to forget her grief. 'You will have a cup,' she enquired, 'and a piece of nice cake?'

At this Jim was not unwilling to stay, but Thomas agonizedly plucked his sleeve. Elias's heavy step could be heard on the stairs. Then he came in, quiet and remote-looking. He laid his hand on Thomas's shoulder for a second.

'Do you remember when we used to go to the Empire, Thomas? You and Gwen used to like that Chinaman that made a white pigeon come out of an empty box.'

But Thomas saw that he was not the same Elias, who, though he would wait long hours for the indifferent Gwen like a faithful dog, had been a strutting young man with a determined eye. He was changed now, his shoulders were slackened. She had defeated him after all. Thomas sipped half a cup of tea, but did not touch the cake. He scarcely spoke. Elias kept on reminding him of various happy incidents in the past. That picnic in the mountains, when Elias had scaled the face of a quarry to fetch a blue flower Gwen had fancied. 'Didn't she dare me to get it!' he added, with a strange chuckle in his throat. 'And then she gave it to you!' He sat brooding for a while, his face turned away. Then, to Thomas's renewed terror, he began to weep again, quietly.

The mother, hobbling across to her son, whispered to the two boys. Perhaps they would go now. It was only yesterday her daughter-in-law had died, and the blow was still heavy on her son. She had stiffened herself out of her own abandonment to grief. The boys went to the door in silence. Jim looked reserved and uncommenting.

But outside, in the dark alley, he said: 'I wonder how she came to chuck the bucket! The baby was it?' Receiving no reply, he added with something like pride now: 'My mother's always having them, but she's only abed for three days, she don't die or nothing near it.' Thomas still stumbling silently by his side, he went on: 'Perhaps he'll marry again; he's only a young bloke . . . I never seen a man cry before,' he added in a voice of contempt.

But for Thomas all the night was weeping. The dark alley was an avenue of the dead, the close shuttered houses were tombs. He heard the wind howling, he could feel the cold ghostly prowling of the clouds. Drops of icy rain stung his cheeks. He was shivering. Gwen's face, bound in its white stillness, moved before him like a lost dead moon. It frightened him, he wanted to have no connection with it; he felt his inside sicken. And all the time he wanted to burst into loud howling like the wind, weep like the rain.

'Shall we look for more?' Jim said. A roused, unappeased appetite was in his voice.

Thomas leaned against the wet wall of a house. Something broke in him. He put up his arm, buried his head in it, and cried. He cried in terror, in fear and in grief. There was something horrible in the dark world. A soft howling whine came out of his throat. Jim, ashamed, passed from wonder into contempt.

'What's up with you!' he jeered. 'You seen plenty of 'em before, haven't you? . . . Shut up,' he hissed angrily. 'There's someone coming.' And he gave Thomas a push.

Thomas hit out. All the world was jangled and threatening and hostile. The back of his hand caught Jim sharply on the cheek-bone. Immediately there was a scuffle. But it was short-lived. They had rolled into a pool of liquidly thin mud, and both were surprised and frightened by the mess they were in.

'Jesus,' exclaimed Jim. 'I'll cop it for this.'

Thomas lurched away. He stalked into the rough night. All about him was a new kingdom. Desperately he tried to think of something else. Of holidays by the sea, of Christmas, of the nut-trees in a vale over the mountains, where, too, thrushes' nests could be found in the spring, marvellously coloured eggs in them. Jim, who had seen him weep, he thought of with anger and dislike.

At the top of the hill leading to his home he paused in anguish. The bare high place was open to the hostile heavens, a lump of earth open like a helpless face to the blows of the wind and the rain. He heard derision in the howls of the wind, he felt hate and anger in the stings of the rain.

A Finger in Every Pie (1942)

The Last Struggle

Grief for the newly-dead is natural in the living and thought of legacies and insurance money to be drawn from them comes second in most persons. Megan Pugh, wife of Sam Two Fingers, thought of the insurance on her husband first, that day when the pit under-manager came to her in person and sat in her kitchen telling her that all hope of rescuing Sam and the other two entombed miners had been abandoned. Megan managed to pull a face. But already her mind was wandering in speculation. A pity she would have to wear black for a time. There was a cerise dress in the window of Lewis Paris House that she madly coveted.

'The water it is,' mourned Mr Rowlands; 'they must have been drowned.' He avoided even thinking that the three men were very likely more horribly obliterated; drowning sounded ordinary. 'Can't get at them,' he mumbled, 'for weeks, p'raps never. Blocks of stone nearly as big as a house and water running under all the time; might cause a flood of the mine if we blast the stone.' There had been a big collapse of roof four days before; four days the men had been entombed.

Fifty pounds Sam was insured for, with the Globe and Atlas people whose New Year gift calendar was on the wall; and of course there would be the compensation money from the pit too. She could go to the seaside; she could even live away from the valley at last. and why should she wear black! Black made her look sallow.

Perhaps, in a way, it was only natural that Megan should be so unnatural. Sam had always kept her short of money; you couldn't hold him off the dogs, though much of a drinker he was not and he had never hit her. He was known as Sam Two Fingers because after a previous accident in the pit one hand was left with the other fingers gone. The strange thing was those two fingers developed a peculiar iron grip.

Only a few months before she had married him – a couple of years ago it was they had hurried to the chapel – she felt it was a mistake; a false alarm the wedding had been. As a courter he had strutted cockily at her side and she took it as pleasure in being in her company. As a married man he had got bossy at once and, when she complained that he was never in the house, answered: 'You can't bring a dog race to the house, can you? Don't I sleep tidy at home every night? What more you want?'

She wanted to be taken about by him, she wanted clothes and train journeys; she did not want to become like the dumpy women of the valley, who only left their doors to go to the shops and the chapel. They had quarrelled like hell. But even in those two years she had been defeated. The valley was a man's valley, with pubs, clubs, dog tracks and football grounds for men only. Perhaps this would change if women went down to work in the pits. But not yet.

'The Company will give you compensation, I dare say,' Mr Rowlands mumbled in embarrassment, thinking her far-away look meant shock or worry.

'How much?' she asked.

Mr Rowlands shook his head. 'An inquest and an enquiry there'll have to be before anything is settled.' He was tired and grey from worry, but tough from long experience of these incidents. Thank goodness, though, Sam Two Fingers's wife didn't make a scene, as some wives did, especially the young ones. He heaved himself up to make the other two calls with the sad news. In their black tomb the men were lying beyond the fret of the living, sealed away for ever from the numerous details and costs of this world. Megan Pugh had sense. She did not cry out for the remains to be found and re-buried in a proper funeral.

Megan locked her front door after him. She did not want neighbours coming in to condole. There were many things to plan. She was tied in no way. Not a child to delay her. The empty days were over. Next morning she was up early and by half-past nine was sitting in a tram-car which linked the districts, colliery by colliery, of the long crab-coloured valley. The July sun shone. It would be nice by the sea if this weather kept.

At the valley's end, in a cottage overlooking the railway, she knocked at a door. It belonged to her Uncle Dai, a greaser on the railway and a private bookie. Dai was no fool with his money but could be persuaded. His wife made a cup of tea when she heard the news and, taking her cue from Megan's lack of tearful display, asked: 'What your plans now?' For Megan still had a gloss on her, knew how to wear a hat, and was a good-looker with skin and teeth still fresh as daisies.

'A little rest straight away,' Megan replied; 'a little rest by myself in Weston-super-Mare, to think things out.'

'Get married more careful next time,' Dai's wife said shrewdly.

'I've been locked up!' Megan said with violence.

'Aye, a regular old Tory your Sam was. A wife was set final for him and couldn't be broke away.'

Dai came in for his dinner at twelve. He made more money as a quiet bookie than as a greaser and did not dislike his niece. Megan produced the insurance book out of her bag and all the weekly payments for Sam were down regular.

'And there's the compensation from the pit too,' she added. 'Mrs Bevan near me had a couple of hundred pounds when her Emlyn got killed.'

She was asking her uncle for an immediate loan of fifty pounds, since very likely, what with inquests and fusses, it would be a week or more before the insurance people paid out. For this favour she was willing to pay him two pounds interest. He could keep the insurance book for security and she would see the insurance agent and tell him that her Uncle Dai was handling her affairs. She wanted to go to Weston-super-Mare without delay; her nerves were upset from the shock.

The chance of making a couple of pounds on such a certain deal made even Dai joke: 'A fancy piece of goods in trousers you got in Weston-super-Mare, Megan? Well, well—'

So, bad though it looked, she skulked off the next day. She took train to the seaside town the other side of the Bristol Channel, did not jib at the high charge in a boarding-house, and then went at once to the drapers' shops and spent ten pounds in an hour. Her most daring purchases, owing to their colour, were a scarlet frock with handbag to match. For three days she lived in the shops and began to believe in happiness again. It was not until the Sunday that she felt appeased and, examining the beach and pier, began to wonder if she had come to the English town to look at men who did not work down under. For she would never marry another miner, coming home black and bellicose from dirty pits.

Weston-super-Mare, in the season, is bright. She

sat eating striped ice-cream and one afternoon she went to Cheddar to visit the famous caves. She kept herself to herself but noticed a man looking at her instead of at the crystal grottoes and stalactites. And in the coach going back there he was sitting next to her! They got talking. He said he was from Birmingham, but he belittled the caves and said there were much finer ones in India.

A quiet-looking chap he was, chatting quite sedate. Malaria had sent him back from India. He was an electrician and had a job in a Birmingham factory now. His lean, lonely appearance was of one who wants looking after, but he ushered her out of the high plush coach with polite confidence. She accepted his invitation to take a glass of something in the lounge of a hotel on the front.

At the end of the second week she told him, grandly: 'I am a widow. Husband killed in the pits at home. But I got a bit of property. Independent.' She wished to be respected and she sounded short.

'Well,' Ted Cricks said, 'that's fine. Look here, I got to go back on Monday. But I dare say I could do a weekend soon as you get home, if asked. Is there a pub I could stay at there?'

She got a bit flustered, thinking of the neighbours. But, sitting on a golden beach with the sky blue and music coming from the pier, the world seemed easy. The tide was rolling in, moving with dark but careless force. She gave him her address and invited him for a weekend. He could sleep at her Uncle Dai's. He said he would wire her from Birmingham.

'Back soon, lovely weather,' was all she had said on the postcard she had sent to Uncle Dai. Forty pounds had been spent and her new suitcase was full. She stayed a few more days. After all, there was the compensation money to come, and she had a houseful of furniture, to say nothing of a promising courter from Birmingham.

On the way back she stopped in Cardiff for an hour and drank three ruby ports in farewell of the triumphant holiday. Wearing her red dress she arrived in the valley at dusk with three pounds in her handbag. But she tossed her head at the valley and admired herself for the flaunting display she was making. It was time some woman showed a respect for her own wants in this place. She did not care what the neighbours, stern guardians of the inexorable laws of the hearth, would think of the gay clothes. Sam wasn't worth mourning, the way he had treated her. She had a good mind to march into a pub there and then and scandalise those entirely male haunts.

As it happened there was no one about in her street. Preened and sunburnt, she unlocked her door. In the dusky passageway she paused just behind the door. Was that the sound of mice? Then her head hung forward and she dropped her red handbag.

The kitchen door at the end of the passage was slowly opening. A two-fingered hand came round it. She could see it distinctly in the twilight. But she could not scream. Her knees like water, she was squatting to the floor. But her face was stretched up, stiffly gazing. The door had been pushed wide open and the ghost of Sam, grey and silent, stood looking at her.

Just the same as when he sat before the fire for a while after his evening bath, before going off to the dogs, he wore trousers and sleeve-rolled shirt, a loose belt round his middle. But his cheeks were hollow and his eyes burned. It was Sam and it wasn't. And from the look of those smouldering eyes she could not move. They stood looking at each other for an age. Suddenly the ghost breathed, far away:

'You get up from there!'

'Sam . . .' she whimpered at last.

'I'll Sam you!' he panted now. 'I'll give you Weston-super-mare . . .' But she had fainted.

To her dying day Megan thought she would never forget those two fingers coming round the door. It had burned into her mind. She found herself lying on the kitchen sofa. The strange thing was that he did not attack her either with tongue or hand. He only looked at her now and again. But for her it was a dead man looking at her. He was still grey from his burial, and thinner, and in his eyes lurked the stagnant glow of one not yet fully back in the world.

'You . . . ' she whispered, 'you were rescued?'

'Aye, I was rescued,' he replied, stern. 'The only one.'

For, when the cracks had sounded in the roofing, he had leapt to a manhole in the facing, a pick-axe in his hand. Two huge blocks of stone from the falling roof had sealed him in there neatly as in an upright coffin. He heard the rush of water and waited to be choked. But the water found a channel away from the manhole and it had faded to a trickling sound. And then time too had faded. The pick's wooden handle had been caught by the edge of the stone and he could not budge it in the narrow space. He had gnawed it through with his teeth, but how long this had taken he did not know, for he had slept, waking again and again to resume the gnawing. He swallowed the chewed-off wood. On the floor was a puddle of gritty water which he managed to scoop up with his hand. At last he could wrench away a stump of the handle. He had thumped with it against the stone for hours, for days, waking from sleep. The miracle had happened at last: they heard the ghostly tapping. By the time they reached him he was unconscious. But after attention he came to with a grunt. Sam Two Fingers was tough as a mule.

She did not ask for the history of his return. She

only whimpered from the sofa: 'I want to go to bed.'

'Aye,' he said briefly, 'go on.'

She rose, swayed, but huddled herself to the door. He stood, looking taller in his leanness, and watched her from those resurrected eyes.

'A red dress!' was all he said. 'No mourning for me!'

He lay at her side in bed like a stranger, not moving. Even his breathing was different; soft it was, as a cat breathes. If only he would touch her she thought her fear would break; once more he would be an alive man. Yet she dreaded that he would touch her with that two-fingered hand. She forced her tongue to say: 'You are sleeping?' He did not answer but she knew he was awake. That night she went down to the last depths of the world. She slept at last and woke to find him gone from her side. And the house was empty, as a house from which a dead person has been removed.

Yet he was downstairs and she smelt something burning. She went down in her nightgown. He had kindled the kitchen fire and was burning her red dress. Under his arm was the handbag. She whispered. 'There's three pound notes in that bag.'

'Not now,' he said. 'Three pounds towards the fifty you got to save.' And he thrust the bag into the fire's core.

Her new suitcase would come up with the

station lorry that morning. She went pale. Thought of the suitcase brought that Birmingham man back to her mind. What was his name? . . . Had that holiday been? She ran upstairs and threw herself on the bed in fright. She did not know his address. But perhaps he would not come, perhaps he had only been playing with her, like they did on holiday. Very likely he was married.

She crept about the house, mechanical at tasks. Sam took very little notice of her, calm in his new power. His only move from the house was to the back lane, where he gossiped with such night-shift men as were hanging about. She had to go to the shops. Women looked at her curiously but no one spoke to her; she kept her eyes down. When she arrived back he was smashing up her suitcase, a look of calm but terrible deliberation in his face.

'Well,' she panted, 'there's foolish!'

'You shut up,' he said. He glanced at her shopping basket. 'You better start saving. Fifty quid you owe your uncle.'

Three days passed just the same, Sam silent but watching her like a cat that seems not to be watching. He never touched her, day or night. Was it that, though physically he was not harmed by his entombment, the shock had unhinged his mind? From him came that new shut-in strength. He had always been bossy and a talkative strutter, but now a deeper and more tenacious power surrounded him so that she felt he was following her even when she went out alone. She wanted to run away, to plead for sanctuary at her Uncle Dai's, screaming that Sam was contemplating some awful punishment, perhaps murder. He showed no signs of returning to work and sat reading a newspaper or book for hours. If only he went to a dog race!

Several times she walked as far as the tram-car stop but always turned back. And there he was still, grey by the fireside, his thick neck bent over a newspaper. If she said something he told her to shut up. But once again he warned her to start saving; he wasn't going to have her beholden to her tyke of an uncle.

'How can I save all that?' she whimpered, but a bit rebellious too.

'Starve yourself,' he barked. 'And if you buy any clothes I'll knock you into the middle of next week.'

Bad luck follows the damned. Sam it was who, when she was out, took in the telegram and opened it. She found the slip of paper on the kitchen table – 'Arriving tomorrow afternoon. Ted.' Sam sat laboriously reading the book by Dickens lent him by a neighbour. He said nothing and she knew by his shoulders that no word could be dragged out of him. She went upstairs and lay on the bed; her stomach was plunging. But presently a new thought came to her and she sat up with a vindictive expression. Now was her chance!

Next day she dressed herself carefully, made up her face, and took several aspirins. She told Sam: 'I've got a visitor coming to tea.'

'Aye,' he said, 'I'll be here.' And turned a page of the maddening book.

'When are you going back to work?' she forced herself to ask.

'You'll know when . . . But I'm not working for you to bloody well pay your uncle fifty quid, see! You got to pay him off your own belly and back, if it takes you ten years.'

'You . . . you devil!' she breathed. But her inside was plunging again. He read on calmly.

There was only one train in the afternoon. She could have met it. But, her face set, she stayed in the house. She did not want Ted to turn back at the station. The kettle was beginning to boil on the fire when the knocker went. Sam still read, sitting in old trousers and shirt-sleeves rolled up; with him a book had to be finished once begun. Her neck throbbing, she closed the kitchen door behind her. Ted stood on the front step with an attaché-case, a new soft hat, and a raincoat neatly folded over his arm. Quite smartly dressed he was, and a man who would make such a long journey to see a holiday pick-up is clearly much attracted. Her confidence grew. 'Hello, Megan,' he said with a kind of nervous jauntiness. 'You never thought I'd come, I bet?'

She smiled gently and quiveringly, the whole appeal of an ill-used woman in it. Her eyes had both hurt and begging. And in the passage she clutched his arm, whimpered a little against his shoulder and let him smell her hair, shampooed that morning. He said, unsteadily: 'Why, what's the matter? . . . There, there now. Have you missed me?'

'Something has happened,' she whispered. 'My husband is here.'

He stiffened. 'But you told me he was dead.'

'It was a mistake. He was rescued after being buried a whole week in the pit . . . Oh, Ted, so cruel he's been to me. I've been going mad. I can't stand it any longer, no indeed I can't.' She clung to his arm.

A call made to a man's gallantry – unless he is of exceptional quality – is rarely left unanswered. Though still bewildered, Ted's face became stern. Having travelled to India he looked upon himself as a man of the world. This dour, ugly coal-mining valley with its harsh look and frowning mountains had depressed him as he walked up from the station. And here was a dainty, tragical little woman chained in it by some ruffian of a husband who was ill-treating her.

All the same, he mumbled cautiously enough: 'Well, do you want me to see him?'

'Yes,' she whispered, in a weak little voice.

'And you want to come away with me?' he asked, a trifle uneasily.

Again she laid her head in trust on his shoulder and breathed: 'Yes.'

Sam looked up from his book when they walked in. The table was laid for tea, very bright and clean, though there was not much food. Sam looked thick, squat and working-man beside Ted's slim but half-wavering height. Megan, standing with her eyes suddenly flashing, said to her husband, who had nodded briefly to the stranger: 'A friend that I met in Weston-super-Mare.'

'Your fancy man, you mean,' Sam grunted, and gave Ted another hard but not dangerous look.

'Will you sit down, Ted?' she asked in an ignoring way, and went to pour water into the teapot.

'You stop that!' barked Sam to her. 'There's no fancy man of my wife going to drink tea in my house.'

'Don't be so silly,' she said unsteadily, and went on pouring water.

He lifted his foot and neatly kicked the pot out of her hand. It smashed on the hearth. Ted involuntarily jumped up, his hat falling from his knee. Megan began whimpering; perhaps her hand was scalded. 'Here!' exclaimed Ted in a peculiar way. Sam sat back in his chair and looked at him squarely. 'What you going to do about it?' he asked, but quite polite.

'He's taking me away!' shouted Megan, enraged. Her face had become twisted and mottled, lips thin as a viper's, eyes hard and menacing. But only for a moment – for she had caught Ted's glance at her. She threw herself whimpering into the sofa, her head lolling woebegone.

Sam, quite calm, told Ted to sit down again. He then addressed the visitor exclusively and with concentration, paying no attention to Megan's sobs: 'Look, here now, Mr What's-your-name, you listen to me . . . You're welcome to her, if you like. She's a bitch but got good points and only wants training – ever had anything to do with greyhounds?' Ted, pale at the gills, shook his head. 'Well,' Sam resumed, 'you don't know they got to be trained, then, and what I'm meaning is that everybody's got to be trained in the same way. Everybody's got to knuckle under some way or another. I got to knuckle under to a lot of sods in the pits, and as I see it a woman's got to knuckle under to a boss of a husband . . . She,' he jerked a thumb towards Megan, 'don't want to and thinks she can break this bloody world's rules and go kicking around with no respect for anything . . . Know what she did soon as she thought I wasn't coming out of that pit alive? Raised fifty quid on my insurance and ran off to Weston-super-Mare without as much as buying a black blouse in mourning of me! That's the sort of woman she is. The old blooming place is talking about it. Why did she do it? All because I go off to the dogs when I've had a day's bellyfull of the pits and don't hang around her neck of evenings like a suckling pig.' His eyes seemed to shoot together in a righteous ferocity. 'She's one of those women that want to make a chap go wobbly at the knees before her, see? Or treat him like a concertina ready for her to play a tune on when she feels like it. She's got to be cured of it, and that's my warning to you.' He slewed a cunning little eye over the startled visitor. 'All the same, she's married to me and I'm not divorcing her, see! But if you want her, there she is and you won't be hearing from me any more.'

Ted had listened to this recital with astonishment and perhaps a bit of fear in his narrow, orderly face. He opened his mouth but closed it again. It was the decisive moment. Suddenly Megan jumped wildly off the sofa.

'You're a bully and a brute,' she flared at Sam. Her fists doubled, she heaved towards him. 'If I was a man I'd knock you down. I don't care if *he* takes me away or not. I'm going to leave you.' Glitteringly she advanced a step further towards him. He looked at her unswervingly but his eyes began to dance. 'You've never been anything else but a mean ruffian, and I hate you. I wish you were rotting now in the pit!' Their gaze was entwined like two flames. She screamed: 'I'm going, I'm going now.'

As if to ward off a blow, he lifted his hand. It was the stumpy two-fingered hand. And she stared at those fingers like someone gone daft. The shadow of a little grin seemed to lurk on his face. But all he said, coolly, was: 'Don't forget your Uncle Dai wants fifty quid off you, and if I know the tyke he'll track you down to the end of the earth for fifty bob!'

Shrinking back, she broke into sobbing and fell once more on to the sofa. 'Why wasn't you killed, why wasn't you killed!' she wept.

Sam turned to the visitor: 'Well, what you going to do? Make up your mind, man. Women don't like mild guts. If you want her, she's there.'

Ted shifted his new hat uneasily from one knee to the other. But he mumbled: 'It can't be done if you won't divorce her.'

'I see you got a respect for the wedding ring,' Sam said approvingly. He added largely: 'Seeing that you thought I was dead I'm not blaming you for chasing a skirt to where you got no business . . . Well,' he raised his voice to the still sobbing Megan, 'seems that your fancy bloke don't want you. Perhaps he thinks you'd do him in for the sake of insurance on him. So you're left on the seashore properly, eh?'

Megan wept: 'I won't be bandied about. Devils

of men. I'll kill myself—' She jumped up again.

'You've brought it on your own head,' Sam barked, very severe. 'What about me, coming back after seven days in my grave and finding my wife gallivanting to the seaside on the insurance money? Expect me to sit down and eat a pork pie as if nothing had happened? By Christ, what about me! I been dead and come alive again and I find the world gone rotten because a woman haven't got even the bit of decency to pull down the blinds and sit wearing a bit of black for me.'

She gazed at him in fear. But for the first time since her return he looked more the old Sam, more alive, as if he was smashing his way through from wherever he had been, that place of stern and ghostly silence. Yet there was something new in him too, something less cocky and more mature. She shrank back from him, and at the same time her body slackened. Her face dwindled and older. She leaned against the dresser, hanging her head.

The visitor rose awkwardly. The room had suddenly filled with a new private tension in which he was cancelled out. He did not know what to say. Sam helped him. 'They'll give you a meal in the Tuberville Arms. Beer there is all right. So long.' Ted went out with a quick sidling movement; even his slim hips, going round the door, looked relieved.

'Done for proper, aren't you!' Sam remarked.

'Fancy man gone, fifty quid in debt, and a cruel husband back from the grave. Well, there's the door. It's a free country.'

'He wasn't ever my fancy man,' she burst out. 'Everything was respectful. We were only interested in each other . . . How was I to know they'd rescue you,' she wailed, 'after Mr Rowlands told me there wasn't any hope!'

'You should have stayed here and gone into mourning properly,' he insisted, severe as a chapel minister. 'Coming back here dressed up in red like a Christmas doll . . . ' His voice began to boil again.

She leaned her head on the dresser shelf and wept again. Hearing him approach she lifted her head and cried out in hysteria, a long irritating howl. It was her last struggle. He gave her a crack on the jaw, not heavy but sufficient to send her against the wall, where she slumped down more in submission than because of the blow. She stopped howling. She saw him not as Sam but as some huge force not to be escaped. He picked her up. His two fingers dug into her back. His mouth caught hers like flame obliterating a piece of paper. She writhed and twisted for a few moments. But she went under, and came to life again.

The Trip to London (1946)

The Public House

Opposite his home was the great public house, a stone building edged with bright yellow bricks. The boy liked the public house. It was clamorous with life, its interior brilliant with coloured bottles and vivid with a harsh smell; the movement of humanity in it interested him. After the staid cleanliness of his home it was satisfying to be allowed entrance, particularly in the early winter evenings, when the pink-speckled gas-lamps were lit and the floor was golden with fresh sawdust and crisp fires burned in the big grates.

He had right of entrance through friendship with the publican's sister, a gaunt spinster of forty who wore much coarse lace about her bodice, a black velvet band firmly binding a high mass of gold hair in which was a strange tint of mildew-green. Generous and lively, she spoke to him in a jokingly rancorous way as if he were grown-up, and gave him pieces of mint-toffee and often a penny. But sometimes she lifted him and stood him on the bar counter, oblivious of the men in the saloon, and, clasping his bare knees with her big moist hands, she would ask him laughingly if he loved her and would he love her always, for ever and for ever. She could make him grin, and because her manner was raucous, he was not offended or humiliated. Yet she made him feel cautious too and he experienced a vague, unformulated feeling when she gripped his knees and, lifting him down from the bar counter, her hand lingered about him. She was a strong woman.

'I don't think the boy ought to get into the habit of going into that public house,' he heard his mother say.

'God bless my soul,' replied his father, 'he's too young to know even what they're for.'

'He'll get so used to a bar—' she went on.

'Well, perhaps he'll go into the business. There's money in pubs, Dorothy. And we'd have brandy and things cost-price, if not for nothing.'

An aloof friendship existed between the two families, though the one was chapel-going and the other, being publicans in the strict Nonconformist place, was cast out in pagan darkness. The ladies gossiped when they met on the pavement and at Christmas exchanged pieces of each other's puddings, one never failing to compliment the other on being more successful than herself. The boy's father, anxious to retain the pub's orders for decoration and painting, sometimes sat on one of its stools and slandered politicians with the publican, a bald widower who looked out on life from the grave of a ruined digestion, eating nothing but frail biscuits and watered-down soups.

'Your boy'll be a preacher,' said the publican, surveying the child, who was kneeling behind the bar rearranging some rows of brown bottles.

'He doesn't look a preacher kneeling down among those stouts,' chuckled the father. 'What makes you think so?'

'His mighty looks at us, as if he's taking us in and finding us wanting.'

Vaguely the boy heard and half understood. He got up from his knees and stared absorbingly at the warm gold of a whisky-bottle. He liked to hold the smooth, cold bottle and shake up the colour. There was the ice-like gin too, and the purple-red of the port, the tawny depths of the sherry; and strange seldom-touched bottles that were startlingly green, white like curdled milk, yellow like buttercups, a red-black like beetroot, and a whitish-gold like sunlight. He stared at them all in turn, lingering for quite two minutes over each. So absorbed was he that he did not see the publican's sister approach and stand, hands on hip, gazing at him as absorbingly.

'Well, my lord, which'll you have?'

He started, pulled from his dream, and saw her huge, gaunt nose thrust out to him, the nostrils twitching with amusement. A sudden feeling of recoil gripped him, so that he was hard and unyielding when she swept when she swept him up into her arms, exclaiming:

'One day you shall have them all. On your wedding-day. You know what that is? Ah! Your wedding-day!'

The power of her physical warmth and dominant voice encircled him. He wriggled and was subjected. She tickled his ribs and he burst into wild laughter. He slipped to the floor and kicked out his legs. When his father, rapping his empty glass on the bar counter, called out: 'Now then, whiskers, time to go home,' he jumped up with great alacrity and ran heading past the rows of stout and out into the hallway. There he joined his father, who was spitting into an enamelled pan marked *Spit Here*. Hand-in-hand they crossed the road and entered the grey evening silence of home.

He liked the public house best on Saturday evenings. Then it was bustling and overflowing with people relaxed from the tension of the finished week and determined to enjoy themselves. It reeked of a life that seemed to sprout with raw vigour like some great healthy cabbage. The windows steamed, all the gas-lamps were ablaze, even the big unappetising 'Commercial Room' was filled with a noisy mob of swollen-faced men. He wriggled his way among a forest of thighs, now and again darting right between a pair of men's legs, accompanied perhaps on these occasions by another boy: they played hide-and-seek among the crowded bodies. The publican's sister had no time for him on Saturday evenings. But sometimes she allowed him to climb on to a chair inside the bar and peer over into that narrow dark section of the pub reserved for women. It was shut-away and secretive, that section, and always shadowy, having no lights of its own. These drinking women fascinated him; they appeared only on Saturday nights; they squatted over their glasses of black stout and talked in low, whining voices; they seemed to hide under large dark hats and they wiped their noses on the backs of their hands. There seemed something mournful aboout them.

Whenever there were apple-fritters Miss Sanders invited him to tea. He ate of them prodigiously, in the sitting-room behind the bar, which, to his great surprise, was like anybody else's sitting-room, containing neither rows of coloured bottles nor sawdust on the floor. Sometimes, after tea, Miss Sanders would play the piano and sing in a deep voice 'Oft in the Stilly Night'. She would then turn to him and say in a bantering way that she sounded like a cockerel. Her voice was a hoarse contralto. Once, when it was time for her to go to the bar, she asked him if he would like to screw on her ear-rings for her, but he was so awkward at the job that she did not repeat the invitation. She smelled of violets and the back of her neck was brown as an autumn leaf. But, in spite of the apple-fritters, he preferred being in the public house proper to sitting there at the back with Miss Sanders.

One afternoon he was playing on the river bank

with another boy. They quarrelled, the boy gave him a push and he fell into the water. His opponent, frightened, ran off. But he had only squelched into some mud, dirtying himself up to his waist. Indignant and alarmed, he gazed in horror at his slimy legs and knickerbockers. How was he to get himself dry and clean before going home! Some particularly unpleasant punishment would be given him if he went home like this. And quickly he thought of his friend Miss Sanders, who never criticised him and would only laugh at his state.

By roundabout back-lane ways, not daring to show himself in the main street, he reached the back of the public house, scrambled up its wall and dropped into the yard. He crept down some steps and peered into the sitting-room window. Yes, she was on the sofa reading a book. He tapped nervously at the window; in his miserable wet state he dared not go to the door. When Miss Sanders had got him inside, her mouth gaped and she screwed up her eyes with laughter.

'Can you,' he stammered, 'can you give me a pan for me to wash my knees? And then I'll stand in front of the fire and get dry.'

She stood in the middle of the room, her arms lifted, both her hands holding the high tower of her green-gold hair; she was looking at him meditatively now, having stopped laughing. 'You come with me,' she said at last. And she patted his head, took his hand and drew him upstairs. The swish of her hard shiny skirts was full of determination.

What a big bathroom they had! And it was white and splendid and not like the poked-away corner of the one in his home. Miss Sanders was turning on the taps in the enormous bath; he did not think anything; he gazed inscrutably before him. Briskly, with quick firm gestures, Miss Sanders took hold of him and whipped off his jersey.

He stood very still but once, as if trapped, he gazed round wildly at the door. Miss Sanders's well-known arms, hard and brisk with power, encircled him. They dexterously peeled off his clothes. He was clammy and shivering, and he was overcome with some strange new feeling that presently solidified into a knot of resentment in his mind. Too late! She had got him into the bath.

She rolled up her sleeves and, telling him that presently they would have some nice hot tea and pineapple together, she soaped him. There was no denying her. Busily, talking all the while with a bright, hard gallop of words, she kneaded and rubbed his flesh. The resentment swelled into anger. At home he washed himself without help now. But he could not bring his tongue to protest. She had the large, high power of the adult, and before this she had always behaved as a friend.

'There now, there now, all white and clean again! My word, look at the water! Eh, your mother would have carried on, I'm glad you came to me first . . . I'll wrap this hot towel round you and you must wear a little jacket of mine till your clothes are dry . . . ' She had lifted him out and was drying him vigorously, kneeling before him now, her breast oppressively against his face.

He did not enjoy his tea, sitting in the woman's jacket. Something had changed. He kept on gazing straight into the bunch of snapdragons on the table, eating with grave austerity and refusing a second helping of pineapple. He was glad when the publican came into the room. When his clothes were dry, Miss Sanders insisted on dressing him. Once she glanced sharply into his face and said:

'You mustn't be frightened, your mother won't be angry now. We won't tell her if you like.'

And she pushed two pennies into his hand. He saw that she was in extraordinary good temper, her grey eyes, under which were mauve patches, bright-eyed as diamonds. The bar was open as he made a slow, almost funereal way through it. A resolve was at the back of his mind but did not declare itself: he made his exit with only a vaguely troubled emotion.

For he never returned to the public house. Daily it was before him, bright and tempting and full of gaiety. He scudded past its steps, kicked a ball on its pavement, played marbles in the road before it. Garlanded with light in the evenings, the piano in the 'Commercial Room' sometimes rollicking out its strident songs, men singing, tales told in the bar, snatches of mysterious phrases over which he used to ponder interestedly – he ignored and forsook them all. He regretted the loss. The public house had been a whole world of marvels and attractive discoveries, and he remembered that part of it with pleasure. And then something happened which made it disagreeable, which ought not to have entered into that particular world. One afternoon as he strolled along the pavement, an upstairs window opened and Miss Sanders popped out her head.

'Hello, there, hello!' she called. 'Why haven't you been to see me lately, you bad boy?'

Hesitating, he looked up but did not answer. She was smiling down at him, a smile of friendly mockery. He remembered thinking that the tower of her hair was in danger of toppling over. She was leaning out in such great eagerness, her bantering smile thrown down to him invitingly. He looked at her with curiosity but had nothing to say. Again asking for an explanation, she added:

'Well, at any rate, come in now. I want to talk to you.'

He did not move. Suddenly she dropped a coin

to him. 'There's sixpence for you!' she cried, her smile breaking into a laugh. 'Now come in to see me.'

Picking up the sixpence, he began to slowly walk away, without comment, even to himself. He only remembered that for a long time he had wanted a certain penknife. Miss Sanders did not call out again, and when he reached the corner he made a sudden headlong dive out of sight.

The Trip to London (1946)

Canute

As the great Saturday drew nearer most men asked each other: 'Going up for the International?' You had the impression that the place would be denuded of its entire male population, as in some archaic tribal war. Of course a few women too intended taking advantage, for other purposes, of the cheap excursion trains, though these hardy souls were not treated seriously, but rather as intruders in an entirely masculine rite. It was to be the eternal England versus Wales battle, the object now under dispute being a stitched leather egg containing an air-inflated bladder.

The special trains began to leave round about Friday midnight, and thereafter, all through the night and until Saturday noon, these quaking, immensely long vehicles feverishly rushed back and forth between Wales and London. In black mining valleys, on rustic heights, in market towns and calm villages myriads of house doors opened during the course of the night and a man issued from an oblong of yellow light, a railway ticket replacing the old spear.

The contingent from Pleasant Row, a respectable road of houses leading up to a three-shafted coalmine, came out from their dwellings into the gas-lit winter midnight more or less simultaneously. Wives stood in worried farewells in the doorways. Their men were setting out in the dead of night to an alien land, far away from this safe valley where little Twlldu nestled about its colliery and usually minded its own business.

'Now be careful you don't lose your head, Rowland!' fretted his wife on their doorstep. 'You take things quiet and behave yourself. Remember your trouble.' The 'trouble' was a hernia, the result of Rowland rescuing his neighbour, Dicky Corner House, from a fall of roof in the pit.

Rowland, grunting a repudiation of this anxiety, scuttled after a group of men in caps. 'Jawl,' shouted one, 'is that the whistle of the 'scursion train? Come on!' Out of the corner house ran Dicky, tying a white muffler round his neck. Weighted though they all were with bottles for the long journey, they shot forward dramatically, though the train was still well up the long valley.

The night was clear and crisp. Thousands of stars briskly gazed down, sleepless as the excited eyes of the excursion hordes thronging all the valley's little stations. Stopping every few minutes, the train slid past mines deserted by their workers and rows of houses where, mostly, only women and children remained. It was already full when it stopped at Twlldu, and, before it left, the smallest men were lying in the luggage-racks and sitting on the floor, placing their bottles safe. Some notorious passengers, clubbing together, had brought crates of flagons.

Dicky Corner House, who was squat and sturdy, kept close to Rowland, offering him cigarettes, or a swig out of his bottle and a beef sandwich. Ever since Rowland had rescued him he had felt bound to him in some way, especially as Rowland, who was not a hefty chap, had that hernia as a result. But Rowland felt no particular interest in Dicky; he had only done his duty by him in the pit. 'Got my own bottle and sandwiches,' he grunted. And: 'No, I am not feeling a draught.' The train rocked and groaned through the historic night. Some parts of it howled with song; in other parts bets were laid, cards played, and tales told of former Internationals.

Somewhere, perhaps guarded by armed warriors, the sacred egg lay waiting for the morrow. In its worship these myriads had left home and loved ones to brave the dangers of a foreign city. Situated in a grimy parish of that city, and going by the name of Paddington, the railway terminus began to receive the first drafts at about 4 a.m. Their arrival was welcomed by their own shouts, whistles and cries. From one compartment next to the Pleasant Row contingent a man had to be dragged out with his legs trailing limply behind him.

'Darro,' Rowland mumbled with some severity, 'he's started early. Disgrace! Gives the 'scursionists a bad name.'

'Hi,' Dicky Corner House tried to hail a vanishing porter, 'where's the nearest public-house in London?'

'Pubs in London opened already then?' asked Shoni Matt in wonder and respect, gazing at 4.30 on the station clock.

'Don't be daft, man,' Ivor snarled, surly from lack of sleep. 'We got about seven hours to wait on our behinds.'

A pitchy black shrouded the great station. Many braved the strange dark and wandered out into it. But in warily peering groups. A watery dawn found their numbers increased in the main thoroughfares; early workers saw them reconnoitring like tribal invaders sniffing out a strange land.

'Well, well,' said Rowland at ten o'clock, following his nose up the length of Nelson's column, 'how did they get that man up there? And what for?'

'A fancy kind of chimney-stack it is,' Dicky declared. 'A big bakehouse is under us.' He asked yet another policeman – the fourth – what time the public houses opened, but the answer was the same.

'Now Dicky,' said Rowland, in a severe canting voice like a preacher, 'you go on behaving like that and very sorry I'll be that I rescued you that time ... We have come here,' he added austerely, 'to see the International, not to drink. Plenty of beer in Wales.'

'I'm cold,' bleated Shoni Matt; 'I'm hungry; I'm sleepy.'

'Let's go in there!' said Gwyn Short Leg, and they all entered the National Gallery, seeing that Admission was Free.

It was the Velasquez *Venus* that arrested their full attention. 'The artist,' observed Emlyn Chrysanthemums – he was called that because he was a prize-grower of them in a home-made glasshouse – 'was clever to make her turn her back on us. A bloke that knew what was tidy.'

'Still,' said Rowland, 'he ought to have thrown a towel or something across her, just by here—'

'Looking so alive it is,' Ivor breathed in admiration, 'you could smack it, just there—'

An attendant said: ' Do not touch the paintings.'

'What's the time?' Dicky Corner House asked the attendant. 'Are the pubs open yet?'

'A disgrace he is,' said Rowland sharply as the contingent went out. 'He ought to have stayed home.'

By then the streets were still more crowded with gazing strangers. Scotland had sent tam-o'-shantered men, the North and Midlands their crowds of tall and short men in caps, bowlers, with umbrellas and striped scarves, concertinas and whistles. There were ghostly-looking men who looked as if they had just risen from hospital beds; others were unshaven and still bore the aspect of running late for the train. Many women accompanied the English contingents, for the Englishman never escapes this. By noon the invaders seemed to have taken possession of the metropolis and, scenting their powerful majority, they became noisy and obstreperous, unlike the first furtive groups which had arrived before dawn. And for a short while a million beer-taps flowed ceaselessly. But few of the visitors loitered to drink overmuch before the match. The evening was to come, when one could sit back released from the tremendous event.

At two-thirty, into a grey misty field surrounded by huge walls of buzzing insects stickily massed together, fifteen red beetles and fifteen white beetles ambled forward on springy legs. To a great cry the sacred egg appeared. A whistle blew. The beetles wove a sharp pattern of movement, pursuing the egg with swift bounds and trim dance evolutions. Sometimes they became knotted over it as though in prayer. They worshipped the egg and yet they did not want it: as if it contained the secret of happiness, they pursued it, got it, and then threw it away. The sticky imprisoning walls heaved and roared; myriads of pin-point faces passed through agonies of horror and ecstasies of bliss. And from a great quantity of these faces came frenzied cries and urgings in a strange primitive language that no doubt gave added strength to the fifteen beetles who understood that language. It was not only the thirty below the walls who fought the battle.

The big clock's pallid face, which said it was a quarter to midnight, stared over the station like an amazed moon. Directly under it was a group of women who had arranged to meet their men there for the journey back. They looked worried and frightened.

And well they might. For surely they were standing in a gigantic hospital-base adjacent to a bloody battlefield where a crushing defeat had been sustained. On the platforms casualties lay groaning or silently dazed; benches were packed with huddled men, limbs twitching, heads laid on neighbours' shoulders or clasped in hands between knees. Trolleys were heaped with what looked like the dead. Now and again an ambulance train crawled out packed to the doors. But still more men kept staggering into the station from the maw of an underground cavern and from the black foggy streets. Most of them looked exhausted, if not positively wounded, as from tremendous strife.

But not all of them. Despite groans of the incapacitated, grunting heaves of the sick, long solemn stares of the bemused helplessly waiting for some ministering angel to conduct them to a train, there was a singing. Valiant groups of men put their heads doggedly together and burst into heroic song. They belonged to a race that, whatever the cause, never ceases to sing, and those competent to judge declare this singing something to be greatly admired. Tonight, in this melancholy place at the low hour of midnight, these melodious cries made the spirit of man seem undefeated. Stricken figures on floors, benches and trolleys stirred a little, and far-gone faces flickered into momentary awareness. Others who still retained their faculties sufficiently to recognise home acquaintances shouted, embraced, hit each other, made excited turkey-cock enquiries as to the activities of the evening.

A youngish woman with parcels picked a zigzag way to under the clock and greeted another there. 'Seen my Glynne, have you?' she asked anxiously; 'I've been out to Cricklewood to visit my auntie . . . Who won the match?' she asked, glancing about her in fear.

'You can tell by the state of them, can't you!' frowned the other.

Another woman, with a heave of hostility, said: 'Though even if Wales had lost they'd drink just the same, to drown the disappointment, the old beasts . . . Look out!' The women scattered hastily from a figure who became detached from a knot of swaying men, made a blind plunge in their direction, and was sick.

'Where's the porters?' wailed one woman. 'There's no porters to be seen anywhere; they've all run home . . . Serve us right, we shouldn't have come with the men's 'scursion . . . I'm feeling ill, nowhere to sit, only men everywhere.'

Cap pushed back from his blue-marked miner's face, Matt Griffiths of Gelli bellowed a way up No. 1 platform. He was gallantly pulling a trolley heaped with bodies like immense dead cods. 'Where's the backwards 'scursion train for Gelli?' he shouted. 'Out of the way there! We got to go on the night-shift tomorrow.'

'The wonder is,' said a woman, fretful, 'that they can find their way to the station at all. But, there, they're like dogs pointing their snouts towards home.'

Two theological students, solemn-clothed as crows, passed under the clock. They were in fierce converse and gesticulated dangerously with their flappy umbrellas. Yet they seemed oblivious of the carnal scenes around them; no doubt they were occupied with some knotty Biblical matter. The huddled women looked at them with relief; here was safety. We'd better get in the same compartment as them,' one of them said to her friend, 'come on, Gwen, let's follow them. I expect they've been up for a conference or an exam.' Soon the two young preachers-to-be were being followed by quite a band of women though they remained unconscious of this flattering retinue.

'That reverse pass of Williams!' one of the students suddenly burst out, unable to contain himself, and prancing forward in intoxicated delight. 'All the matches I've been to I've never seen anything like it! Makes you want to grab someone and dance ring-a-ring o'roses.'

Elsewhere, an entwined group of young men sang *Mochyn Du* with an orderly sweetness in striking contrast to their mien; a flavour of pure green hills and neat little farmhouses was in their song about a black pig. On adjacent platforms other groups in that victorious concourse sang *Sospan Fach* and even a hymn. As someone said, if you shut your eyes you could fancy yourself in an eisteddfod.

But in the Gentlemen's Convenience under No. 1 platform no one would have fancied this. There an unusual thing had occurred – the drains had clogged. Men kept on descending the flight of steps only to find a sheet of water flooding the floor to a depth of several inches. They had to make-do with standing on the bottom steps, behind them an impatient block of others dangerously swaying.

And this was not all. Far within the deserted convenience one man was marooned over that sheet of water. He sat on the shoe-shine throne which, resting on its dais, was raised safely – up to the present – above the water. Astonished remarks from the steps failed to reach him.

'Darro me,' exclaimed one man with a stare of respect across the waters, 'how did he get there? No sign of a boat.'

'Hoy,' another bawled over, 'what train you want to catch? You can't stay there all night.'

'Who does he think he is,' someone exclaimed in an English voice – 'King Canute?'

The figure did not hear, though the head dreamily lolled forward an inch. Impatient men waiting on the crowded steps bawled to those in front to hurry up and make room. Soon the rumour that King Canute was sitting below passed among a lot of people on No. 1 platform. It was not long before someone – Sam Recitations it was, the Smoking Concert Elocutionist – arrived at the bottom step and recognised that the figure enthroned above the water was not King Canute at all.

'I'm hanged if it isn't Rowland from Pleasant Row!' he blew in astonishment. 'That's where he's got! . . . Rowland,' his chest rose as in a recitation, 'wake up, man, wake up! Train is due out in ten minutes. Number 2 platform . . . '

Rowland did not hear even this well-known Twlldu voice. Sam himself not in full possession of his faculties, gazed stupidly at the sheet of water. it looked deep; up to your calves. A chap would have soaking wet socks and shoes all the way back to Wales. And he was appearing at a club concert on Tuesday, reciting four ballads; couldn't afford to catch a cold. Suddenly he pushed his way through the exclaiming mob behind him, hastened recklessly through the platform mobs, reached No. 2 platform and began searching for the Pleasant Row contingent.

They were sitting against a kiosk plunged in torpid thought. Sam had to shake two or three of them. 'I've seen him!' he rolled. 'Your Rowland! He isn't lost – he's down in the men's place under Number 1, and can't budge him. People calling him King Canute—'

They had lost him round about nine o'clock in crowded Trafalgar Square. There the visiting mob had got so obstreperous that, as someone related later at a club in Twlldu, four roaring lions had been let loose and stood lashing their tails in fury against these invaders whose nation had won the match; and someone else said that for the first time in his life he had seen a policeman who wore spectacles. While singing was going on, and two or three cases of assault brewing, Rowland had vanished. From time to time the others had missed him, and Dicky Corner House asked many policemen if they had seen Rowland of Twlldu.

Sam Recitations kept on urging them now.

'King Canute?' repeated Shoni Matt in a stupor. 'You shut up, Sam,' he added crossly: 'no time for recitations now.'

'He's down in the Gents under Number 1,' Sam howled despairingly. 'English strangers poking fun at him and water rising up! He'll be drowned same as when the Cambrian pit was flooded!' He beat his chest as if he was giving a ballad in a concert. 'Ten minutes and the train will be in! And poor Rowland sitting helpless and the water rising round him like on the sands of Dee!'

Far off a whistle blew. Someone near by was singing *Cwm Rhondda* in a bass that must have won medals in its time. They shook themselves up from the platform, staring penetratingly at Sam, who was repeating information with wild emphasis. Six of them, all from Pleasant Row. Awareness seemed to flood them simultaneously, for suddenly they all surged away.

By dint of pushing and threatening cries they got down all together to the lower steps of the Convenience. Rowland had not moved in the shoe-shine throne. Still his head lolled in slumber as if he was sitting cosy by his fireside at home after a heavy shift in the pit, while the waters lapped the dais and a yellow light beat down on the isolated figure indifferent to its danger. They stared fearfully at the sheet of water.

'Shocking it is,' said Gwyn Short Leg,

scandalised. 'All the Railway Company gone home, have they, and left the place like this?'

'In London too!' criticised Ivor, gazing below him in owlish distaste.

Then in one accord they bellowed: 'Hoy, Rowland, hoy!'

He did not stir. Not an eyelid. It was then that Shoni Matt turned to Dicky Corner House and just looked at him, like a judge. His gaze asked – 'whose life had been saved by Rowland when that bit of roof had fallen in the pit?' Dicky, though he shivered, understood the long solemn look. 'Time to pay back now, Dicky,' the look added soberly.

Whimpering, Dicky tried to reach his shoelaces, on the crowded steps. But the others urged excitedly: 'No time to take your shoes off. Hark, the train's coming in! Go on, boy. No swimming to do.'

Dicky, with a sudden dramatic cry, leapt into the water, foolishly splashing it up all round his legs. A pit-butty needed to be rescued! And with oblivious steps, encouraged by the applause of the others, he plunged across to the throne. He stepped on the dais and, being hefty, lifted Rowland across his shoulders without much bother. He staggered a bit as he stepped off the dais into the cruelly wet water.

'Careful now,' shouted Emlyn Chrysanthemums; 'don't drop him into the champagne.'

It was an heroic act that afterwards, in the club

evenings, took precedence over tales of far more difficult rescues in the pits. Dicky reached the willing arms of the others without mishap. They took Rowland and bore him by his four limbs up the steps, down the platform and up the other, just as the incoming train was coming to a frightened standstill. After a battle they got into a compartment. Dicky took off his shoes, hung up his socks over the edge of the track and wiped his feet and calves in the white muffler that had crossed his throat.

'Wet feet bad for the chest, ' he said fussily.

All the returning trains reached the arms of Wales safely, and she folded the passengers into her fragrant breast with a pleased sigh of 'Well done, my sons'. The victory over her ancient enemy – it was six points to four – was a matter of great Sunday celebration when the men's clubs opened in the evening, these having a seven-day licence, whereas the ordinary public houses, owing to the need to appease old dim gods, were not allowed to open on Sundays.

The members of the Pleasant Row contingent, like most others, stayed in bed all the morning. When they got up they related to their wives and children many of the sights and marvels of London. But some weeks had passed before Rowland's wife, a tidy woman who starched her aprons and was a great chapel-goer, said to him in perplexity: 'Why is it people are calling you Rowland Canute now?'

Only that evening, Gwyn Short Leg, stumping to the door on his way to the club, had bawled innocently into the passage: 'Coming down, Rowland Canute?' Up to lately Rowland had been one of those who, because he seemed to have no peculiarity, had never earned a nickname.

'Oh,' Rowland told his wife, vaguely offhand, 'some fancy name or other it is they've begun calling me.'

'But a reason there must be for it,' she said inquisitively. 'Canute! Wasn't that some old king who sat on his throne beside the sea and dared the tide to come over him? A funny name to call you.'

'What you got in that oven for my supper?' he asked, scowling at the news in the evening paper.

She knew better than to proceed with the matter just then. But of course she did not let it rest. It was the wife of Emlyn Chrysanthemums, living three doors up, who, in the deprecating way of women versus the ways of men, told her the reason. There are nicknames which are earned respectably and naturally, and indeed such nicknames are essential to identify persons in a land where there are only twenty or so proper baptised names for everybody. But, on hearing how Rowland earned Canute, his wife pursed in her lips like a pale tulip, opening them hours later to shout as Rowland tramped in from the pit:

'Ah, *Canute* is it! . . . Sitting there in that London place,' she screamed, 'and all those men—' She whipped about like a hailstorm. 'You think I'm going to stay in Twlldu to be called Mrs Rowland Canute, do you? We'll have to move from here – you begin looking for work in one of the other valleys at once.'

And such a dance she led him that in a couple of months they had left Pleasant Row. Rowland got taken on at the Powell pit in the Cwm Mardy valley, several stout mountains lying between that and Twlldu.

Yet give a dog a bad name, says the proverb, and it will stick. Who could have thought that Sam Recitations, growing in fame, would visit a club in far-away Cwm Mardy to give selections from his repertoire at a Smoking Concert? And almost the first man he saw when he entered the bar-room was Rowland. 'Why now,' his voice rolled in delight, 'if it isn't Rowland Canute! Ha, ha—' And not noticing Rowland's dropped jaw of dismay, he turned and told all the clustering men what had happened under Paddington platform that time after the famous International – just as the history of the rescue had been told in all the clubs in the valley away over the mountains.

Boy with a Trumpet (1949)

Fear

As soon as the boy got into the compartment he felt there was something queer in it. The only other occupant was a slight, dusky man who sat in a corner with that air of propriety and unassertiveness which his race – he looked like an Indian – tend to display in England. There was also a faint sickly scent. For years afterwards, whenever he smelled that musk odour again, the terror of this afternoon came back to him.

He went to the other end of the compartment, sat in the opposite corner. There were no corridors in these local trains. The man looked at him and smiled friendlily. The boy returned the smile briefly, not quite knowing what he was thinking, only aware of a deep, vague unease. But it would look so silly to jump out of the compartment now. The train gave a jerk and began to move.

Then, immediately with the jerk, the man began to utter a low humming chant, slow but with a definite rhythm. His lips did not open or even move, yet the hum penetrated above the noise of the train's wheels. It was in a sort of dreamy rhythm, enticing, lonely and antique; it suggested monotonous deserts, an eternal patience, a soothing wisdom. It went on and on. It was the kind of archaic chant that brings to the mind images of slowly swaying bodies in some endless ceremony in a barbaric temple.

Startled, and very alive to this proof of there being something odd in the compartment, the boy turned from staring out of the window – already the train was deep in the country among lonely fields and dark wooded slopes – and forced himself to glance at the man.

The man was looking at him. They faced each other across the compartment's length. Something coiled up in the boy. It was as if his soul took primitive fear and crouched to hide. The man's brown lips became stretched in a mysterious smile, though that humming chant continued, wordlessly swaying out of his mouth. His eyes, dark and unfathomable, never moved from the boy. The musk scent was stronger.

Yet this was not all. The boy could not imagine what other fearful thing lurked in the compartment. But he seemed to sense a secret power of something evilly antipathetic. Did it come from the man's long pinky-brown hands, the sinewy but fleshless hands of a sun-scorched race? Long tribal hands like claws. Or only from the fact that the man was of a far country whose ways were utterly alien to ours? And he continued to smile. A faint and subtle smile, while his eyes surveyed the boy as if he contemplated action. Something had flickered in and out of those shadowy eyes, like a dancing malice.

The boy sat stiffly. Somehow he could not return to his staring out of the window. But he tried not to look at the man again. The humming did not stop. And suddenly it took a higher note, like an unhurried wail, yet keeping within its strict and narrow compass. A liquid exultance wavered in and out of the wail. The noise of the train, the flying fields and woods, even the walls of the compartment, had vanished. There was only this chant, the man who was uttering it, and himself. He did not know that now he could not move his eyes from those of the man.

Abruptly the compartment was plunged into blackness. There was a shrieking rush of air. The train had entered a tunnel. With a sudden jerk the boy crouched down. He coiled into the seat's corner, shuddering, yet with every sense electrically alive now.

Then, above the roar of the air and the hurling grind of the train, that hum rose, dominantly establishing its insidious power. It called, it unhurriedly exhorted obedience, it soothed. Again it seemed to obliterate the louder, harsher noises. Spent and defeated, helplessly awaiting whatever menace lay in the darkness, the boy crouched. He knew the man's eyes were gazing towards him; he thought he saw their gleam triumphantly piercing the darkness. What was this strange presence of evil in the air, stronger now in the dark?

Suddenly crashing into the compartment, the hard blue and white daylight was like a blow. The train had gained speed in the tunnel and now hurled on through the light with the same agonising impetus, as if it would rush on for ever. Spent in the dread which had almost cancelled out his senses, the boy stared dully at the man. Still he seemed to hear the humming, though actually it had ceased. He saw the man's lips part in a full enticing smile, he saw teeth dazzlingly white between the dusky lips.

'You not like dark tunnel?' The smile continued seductively; once more the flecks of light danced wickedly in his eyes. 'Come!' He beckoned with a long wrinkled finger.

The boy did not move.

'You like pomegranates?' He rose and took from the luggage-rack a brown wicker basket. It was the kind of basket in which a large cat would be sent on a journey. 'Come!' he smiled friendlily and, as the boy still did not move, he crossed over and sat down beside him, but leaving a polite distance.

The staring boy did not flinch.

'Pomegranates from the East! English boy like, eh?' There seemed a collaboration in his intimate voice; he too was a boy going to share fruit with his friend. 'Nice pomegranates,' he smiled with good-humour. There was also something stupid in his manner, a fatuous mysteriousness.

The basket lay on his knees. He began to hum again. The boy watched, still without movement, cold and abstract in his non-apprehension of this friendliness. But he was aware of the sickly perfume beside him and, more pronounced than ever, of an insidious presence that was utterly alien. That evil power lay in his immediate vicinity. The man looked at him again and, still humming, drew a rod and lifted the basket's lid.

There was no glow of magically gleaming fruits, no yellow-and-rose-tinted rinds enclosing honeycombs of luscious seeds. But from the basket's depth rose the head of a snake. It rose slowly to the enchantment of the hum. It rose from its sleepy coil, rearing its long brownish-gold throat dreamily, the head swaying out in languor towards the man's lips. Its eyes seemed to look blindly at nothing. It was a cobra.

Something happened to the boy. An old warning of the muscles and the vulnerable flesh. He leapt and flung himself headlong across the compartment. He was not aware that he gave a sharp shriek. He curled against the opposite seat's back, his knees pressing into the cushion. But, half turning, his eyes could not tear themselves from that reared head.

And it was with other senses that he knew most deeply he had evoked rage. The cobra was writhing in disturbed anger, shooting its head in his direction. He saw wakened pin-point eyes of black malice. More fearful was the dilation of the throat, its skin swelling evilly into a hood in which shone two palpitating sparks. In some cell of his being he knew that the hood was swelling in destructive fury. He became very still.

The man did not stop humming. But now his narrowed eyes were focused in glittering concentration on the snake. And into that hum had crept a new note of tenacious decision. It was a pitting of subtle power against the snake's wishes and it was also an appeasement. A man was addressing a snake. He was offering a snake tribute and acknowledgement of its right to anger; he was honeyed and soothing. At the same time he did not relax an announcement of being master. There was courtesy towards one of the supreme powers of the animal kingdom, but also there was the ancient pride of man's supremacy.

And the snake was pacified. Its strange reared collar of skin sank bank into its neck; its head ceased to lunge towards the boy. The humming slackened into a dreamy lullaby. Narrowly intent now, the man's eyes did not move. The length of tawny body slowly sank back. Its skin had a dull glisten, the glisten of an unhealthy torpidity. Now the snake looked effete, shorn of its venomous power. The drugged head sank. Unhurriedly the man closed the basket and slipped its rod secure.

He turned angrily to the boy; he made a contemptuous sound, like a hiss. 'I show you cobra and you jump and shout, heh! Make him angry!' There was more rebuke than real anger in his exclamations. But also his brown face was puckered in a kind of childish stupidity; he might have been another boy of twelve. 'I give you free performance with cobra, and you jump and scream like little girl.' The indignation died out of his eyes; they became focused in a more adult perception. 'I sing to keep cobra quiet in train,' he explained. 'Cobra not like train.'

The boy had not stirred. 'You not like cobra?' the man asked in injured surprise. 'Nice snake now, no poison! But not liking you jump and shout.'

There was no reply or movement; centuries and continents lay between him and the boy's still repudiation. The man gazed at him in silence and added worriedly: 'You going to fair in Newport? You see me? Ali the Snake Charmer. You come in free and make cobra dance—'

But the train was drawing into the station. It was not the boy's station. He made a sudden blind leap away from the man, opened the door, saw it was not on the platform side, but jumped. There was a shout from someone. He ran up the track, he dived under some wire railings. He ran with amazingly quick short leaps up a field – like a hare that knows its life is precarious among the colossal dangers of the open world and has suddenly sensed one of them.

Boy with a Trumpet (1949)

For further reading

Novels
Except for the posthumous novel *Ram with Red Horns* (Seren, 1996), all Rhys Davies's novels are out of print, but they can often be found in secondhand bookshops; they include: *A Time to Laugh* (1937), *Jubilee Blues* (1937), *Under the Rose* (1940), *Tomorrow to Fresh Woods* (1941), *The Black Venus* (1944), *The Dark Daughters* (1947), *Marianne* (1951), *The Painted King* (1954), *The Perishable Quality* (1957), *Girl Waiting in the Shade* (1960), *Nobody Answered the Bell* (1971), and *Honeysuckle Girl* (1975); all these were published by Heinemann.

Short Stories
Meic Stephens (ed.), *The Collected Stories of Rhys Davies* (Gomer, 3 vols., 1996, 1998)

Autobiography
Print of a Hare's Foot (Heinemann, 1969; new edn. Seren, 1998)

Criticism
David Rees, *Rhys Davies*, a monograph in the *Writers of Wales* series (University of Wales Press, 1975)
Meic Stephens (ed.), *Rhys Davies: Decoding the Hare* (University of Wales Press, 2001)

Images of Wales

The Corgi Series covers, no.10
'From Flat 11 no.5' by Ernest Zobole; oil on canvas; 123 x 153 cm; 1988 (supplied by kind permission of Professor Tony Curtis and the Ernest Zobole Art Collection, University of Glamorgan)

Ernest Zobole (1927-1999)

Ernest Zobole's career as an artist in Wales spanned the whole of the second half of the twentieth century. Throughout this period, he used the Rhondda where he lived to explore and develop his life-long obsession with art and the nature of vision and existence. The outcome was the production of a significant body of visually arresting paintings and works on paper that mark him out as an artist of both Welsh and European standing.

Zobole was born in Ystrad in 1927 and his oil paintings were noticed as early as 1950 by the influential David Bell, who saw Zobole's and his Rhondda Group contemporaries' depictions of the Valleys as part of an embryonic 'Welsh School of Painting'.

From 1960 onwards, Zobole shifted towards a more modern, post-cubist approach whereby the picture was treated as a primarily physical and formal object, on the surface of which new ideas about form, space and time could be worked out.

composition, internal scale and style could be played with. This was followed by a return to a fresh range of strong colours and rich patterns.

However, it is the increasingly dream-like and universalising work from the mid-eighties up to his death in 1999 for which he is now best remembered. These images became a vehicle for his memory and imagination. Interior and exterior views were often combined, and compositions were made more map-like and fragmented. The overall result was a sort of magic realism, but one that was to the very end highly original and still evolving.

Zobole exhibited regularly throughout his career and, in 1992, was the subject of a BBC Wales television documentary entitled *Ernest Zobole: Seeing and Remembering*. Currently his life and works are being researched, recorded and presented at the University of Glamorgan in readiness for the first retrospective exhibition of the artist's work which will tour Wales in 2004-05.

For further information and enquiries, please contact Ceri Thomas:
By email at:
HYPERLINK mailto:cthomas1@glam.ac.uk/
cthomas1@glam.ac.uk
Website: HYPERLINK http://www.glam.ac.uk/
www.glam.ac.uk